# Amazing Grace

**God's loving plan for your life**

E. LONNIE MELASHENKO

**Pacific Press® Publishing Association**
Nampa, Idaho
Oshawa, Ontario, Canada
www.pacificpress.com

Cover design: Michelle C. Petz
Cover images: Copyright © Getty Images


Copyright © 2003 by
Pacific Press® Publishing Association
Printed in the United States of America
All Rights Reserved

Additional copies of this book may be purchased at
www.adventistbookcenter.com


ISBN: 0-8163-1990-1


03  04  05  06  07  •  5  4  3  2  1

# Contents

God's Amazing Grace ..................................................... 7

God's Greatest Gift ..................................................... 17

Grace That Saved ..................................................... 22

A Wretch Like Me ..................................................... 27

I Once Was Lost ..................................................... 32

But Now Am Found ..................................................... 37

I Was Blind ..................................................... 42

Now I See ..................................................... 49

More Than Amazing Grace ..................................................... 55

It's Your Choice ..................................................... 60

# Preface

The ideas in this book have been coming together in my mind and in my ministry for a number of years. None of us will ever be able to fully comprehend God's amazing grace or express it adequately. But we can all experience it personally and know the miracles it can accomplish in our lives.

I want to express my appreciation to David B. Smith, my colleague here at *The Voice of Prophecy,* for the significant contribution he has made to this book. As he and I have worked together, David has helped me formulate and put into words many of the concepts found in this book. I owe much to him and his abilities as a wordsmith. I also want to acknowledge the part played by the many individuals who have written or responded in some way to the radio ministry. Their experiences have enriched my understanding of how God works in human hearts and have been a source of inspiration to me in my own personal walk with the Savior. It is the spiritual struggles of everyday life that shape our understanding of God's amazing grace and its far-reaching effects.

It is my prayer that you will understand more deeply God's great love for you as you read these pages.

Lonnie Melashenko
April 2003

# Introduction

Christians ought to celebrate more. Rejoice in our faith. Nothing honors Jesus more than for us to praise Him and party when we discover God's amazing grace. Luke, chapter 15, relates three grace-oriented stories in which something lost is found: a coin, a sheep, and a son. For each there is a celebration. A party. The point being that Jesus is happiest when the lost are found. No moment compares with praising God in sacred song, praise, prayer, and thanksgiving.

"There is joy in the presence of angels over one sinner that repents" (Luke 15:3). Why such a stir? Why would every heavenly being celebrate over *one sinner* who repents? Heaven throws a party, pours the bubbly, strings streamers, and throws confetti—why? Perhaps we miss the obvious answer. Jesus and the angels see something we can't see behind the scenes: a repentant sinner no longer dressed in rags, but in robes of righteousness. A new child "born again" into heaven's family. God gets so excited He personally gets out His invitation list and orchestrates a great, big, beautiful party, festooned for celebration.

Surprise birthday parties are so much fun! When I reached fifty, I told Jeannie, "Don't do much. A nice quiet evening out with family, perhaps." But first, I tried to talk Jeannie and her mother out of it. "I just want to stay home tonight. Let's go out on another night. Please?"

My objections were met with a united front and a unanimous vote: "You're going. On time."

"Well, OK then. We can meet a few friends in Camarillo." I was unaware fifty families would show up at the church fellowship center.

*They all knew* about the party. Jeannie and her mother and the hundred friends understood what was going on behind the scenes. I didn't. "Why dress up? Do I have to go?" Only when I finally stepped inside did their actions make sense. SURPRISE! Now I, too, saw the table stacked with gifts, smelled the cake, and got caught up in the reverie.

My purpose in writing this book is that I want to do everything necessary to see that people don't miss out on heaven's party. These chapters share God's invitation to His party. There are those who haven't seen the table, haven't heard the music, haven't experienced His amazing grace. And they *must know it*—because it's party time!

# CHAPTER ONE

# God's Amazing Grace

Tony Campolo, Christian writer, pastor, and sociologist, tells of wandering the streets of Honolulu at 3:00 A.M. looking for something to eat. Even in this tourist spot where the flow of pedestrians continues day and night, almost everything was closed. Finally, he found a little "greasy spoon" still open up a side street. Tony went in and sat down on a stool. The place was so filthy, he didn't even want to touch the menu, but he ordered coffee and a doughnut from the fat guy behind the counter. And wished he hadn't when the man handed him a doughnut with his bare grimy hands!

Then as Tony sat munching, the door opened, and to his discomfort in marched eight or nine noisy, boisterous prostitutes. And that wasn't all. They came and sat down on stools beside him! Their conversation was loud and crude. He felt completely out of place and was just about to make his escape, when the woman beside him announced to no one in particular, "Tomorrow's my birthday; I'll be thirty-nine."

"So what," responded her friend nastily. "What do

you want from me? A birthday party? You want me to get you a cake and sing 'Happy Birthday' ?"

"I was just telling you, that's all," the first woman said. "Why are you being so mean? You don't have to put me down. I don't want anything from you. Why should you give me a birthday party? I've never had a birthday party in my whole life; why should I have one now?"

Well, when Tony Campolo heard that, he made a decision right then and there. When the prostitutes left, he turned to the guy behind the counter—his name was Harry—and asked, "Do those women come in here every night?"

"Yeah."

"That one who was sitting right next to me—does she come every night?"

"Yeah. That's Agnes. She comes in every night. Why d'ya wanta know?"

"Because I heard her say tomorrow is her birthday. How about if you and I do something about that? What do you think about us throwing a birthday party for her right here—tomorrow night?"

Harry's eyes lit up. "That's a great idea." He turned to the back room and shouted to the woman there, "Hey! Come out here. This guy's got a great idea. Tomorrow's Agnes's birthday, and this guy wants us to go in with him and throw her a birthday party—right here, tomorrow night!"

Harry's wife came out from the back all bright and smiley. "That's wonderful! Agnes is one of those people who is really nice and kind. Nobody ever does anything nice or kind for her, though."

"Look," Tony said, "if it's OK with you, I'll get back

here tomorrow about 2:30 in the morning and decorate the place. I'll even get a birthday cake!"

"No way," replied Harry. "The birthday cake's my thing. I'll make the cake."

At 2:30, Tony was back with crepe-paper decorations and a cardboard sign saying "Happy Birthday!" He decorated the diner from one end to the other. The woman who did the cooking must have gotten word out on the street because at 3:15 every prostitute in Honolulu was in the place. It was wall-to-wall prostitutes—and Tony Campolo!

At 3:30 on the dot, the door swung open, and in came Agnes with her friend. Tony had everybody ready, and they shouted out, "Happy Birthday!"

Agnes was stunned. Flabbergasted. Shaken. Her mouth fell open, and her legs buckled. As she sat down on a bar stool, everybody sang, "Happy Birthday." Agnes got misty-eyed. When the birthday cake came out, she lost it and began sobbing.

"Blow out the candles, Agnes," Harry mumbled gruffly. "Come on! Blow out the candles! If you don't blow out the candles, *I'm* gonna hafta blow them out." And Harry did end up having to do it.

"Cut the cake, Agnes," Harry continued. "Yo, Agnes! We all want some cake."

Tony prayed. Everyone had a great time. Finally, when Agnes and her friends were gone, Harry leaned over the counter and said, "Hey, you never told me you were a preacher! What kind of church do you belong to?"

Tony said later that it was one of those moments when the right words just seem to come without thinking about it. He replied, "I belong to a church that throws birthday parties for whores at 3:30 in the morning."

Harry waited a moment, then sneered: "No you don't. There's no church like that. If there was, I'd join it. I'd join a church like that!"

Isn't that the kind of church Jesus came to create? Based on the record of when He lived with us on earth, Jesus loved to party with all kinds of left-out people—tax collectors, sinners, lepers, and prostitutes. They all loved Him because He was willing to spend time with them.

But Jesus didn't associate with sinners just out of a sense of duty; He enjoyed their company. He preferred going to parties with the shunned and the looked down on. When the religious leaders and the "good" people confronted Him about partying with sinners, Jesus said, "Quite frankly, I prefer their company to yours!"

## Stories of the lost

In Luke 15, Jesus told three stories about the lost—a lost coin, a lost sheep, and a lost son. All three were lost. But Jesus didn't tell these stories to focus on their "lostness." That wasn't His emphasis at all. He told these stories to emphasize in each case the outrageous joy that took place when they were found! The woman sweeps the floor and lights a lamp to find her lost coin. And when she does, she's thrilled. She calls her friends to celebrate with her. The shepherd searches high and low for his lost sheep. And when he finds it, he brings it home with rejoicing. He's happy! And the father runs to meet his lost son, his heart overflowing with joy and love for his missing boy who has been found at last.

You see, Jesus designed His church to be a *party!* The church is to show the world a thrilling foretaste of what's coming. Knowing Jesus is like a teenager looking forward to a Saturday night date. Remember how that was? In fact, God called the Jews, His Old Testament people, to do precisely that—to give the world a preview of the joy and rejoicing that knowing God brings. Every fiftieth year was to be an outrageous party; they called it the "Jubilee." Debts were canceled; the land returned to its original owners; prisoners were set free; the land was not plowed or worked, and the people lived off the bounty of the previous year. God wanted the heathen to look at His people and say, "Wow! We want in! We want to be a part of God's people too!"

But the Jews never really got into the spirit of what God had in mind for them. It remained for Jesus to do when He came as the Messiah to usher in God's new kingdom.

And God's purpose still remains the same. Whenever His people celebrate and laugh and sing, they are sending out a message, saying, "Good news! The kingdom of God is here, and it's great. It's a lot of fun!" Those outside, looking on, say, "Hey! We want in!"

Of course, critics will always blast away. Someone will always find fault if you make the gospel to be really good news. In fact, Jesus warned that we would be criticized just as He was. The religious leaders of His day found fault with Jesus. "He has a devil," they accused. "He's always eating and drinking with sinners; He's a glutton and a drunk!" (see Matthew 11:16-19). No matter what you do, there will always be faultfinders to pick you apart. These killjoys are never satisfied.

## The world has its parties too

Please notice that we aren't saying that Christians should party like the world parties. The world has its parties too. Extravagant bashes with booze, babes, and boogie. That's not the kind of party that Jesus engaged in; that's not the kind of party He is recommending. The world's parties are cruel and dehumanizing. Empty and impoverished.

God wants His church to be a place where people come to enjoy themselves, to celebrate and praise and sing, and have a good time. Jesus challenges us to become blazingly alive, to allow Him to invade our entire personalities with joy. That's God's radical plan for His family.

In fact, I'd like to suggest that this is why Jesus told the story of the lost son in Luke 15. He wanted to make this very point—that the gospel thrives on celebration and joy.

> The father said to his servants, Bring forth the best robe, and put it on him; and put a ring on his hand, and shoes on his feet: And bring hither the fatted calf, and kill it; and let us eat, and be merry: For this my son was dead, and is alive again; he was lost and is found. And they began to be merry (Luke 15:22-24, KJV).

## The lost son

This lost son—we call him the "prodigal" son—is as rotten a figure in the New Testament as Jesus ever described. It's impossible to overdramatize how deceptive, manipulative, ego-centered, and arrogant he was.

"Dad, I don't like being your son. I wish you were dead! Since you aren't, I want outta' here." Or, as Jesus put it, "The younger one said to his father, 'Father, give me my share of the estate.' So he divided his property between them" (Luke 15:12). And the dad gives the boy what he asks for—one-half of the family fortune!

The son packs his bags and heads his new Corvette straight for Las Vegas. Or, as Jesus put it, "Not long after that, the younger son got together all he had, set off for a distant country and there squandered his wealth in wild living" (verse 13). The Greek words imply that he plunged into the worst kind of sin and immorality possible. He blows the entire bundle on booze, bunnies, bimbos, blackjack, and bubbly burgundy wine. He's living in Glitter Gulch, light years from home on the farm.

But one day at the Vegas slots, the money finally runs out. Suddenly, the young man has no friends. He's sunk to the bottom. He's eating with pigs out of sewers! Notice something profound in verse 17: "And when he came to himself . . ."

As the Holy Spirit spoke to him, as he saw what a mess he had made of his life, he came to himself and said, *What am I doing here? I have no food, no money, no friends, no options! And I created this mess!* You see, he can't blame his friends, his pastor, his school teachers, or his religious-fanatic brother at home. He realizes, *I'm the one to blame. I'm a sinner.* And in his moment of self-realization, he completely gives up!

Verse 17 says that he finally admits to himself, "How many of my father's hired men have food to spare, and here I am starving to death! I will arise and go back to my father and say to him, 'Father, I've sinned against heaven and against you. I am no longer worthy to be called your son; make me like one of your hired men.'" The climax comes in verse 20: "And he arose and came to his father."

Please notice that it does *not* say that he has repented—yet. He hasn't really understood things yet.

Oh, he thinks up a speech. But he's still works-oriented. *I going to go home to work for Dad. I'll qualify to be a servant. I'll knuckle down and earn my keep.* He comes home for one reason—to manipulate the father once more. Because that's the way sin always is. When sinners come to Jesus Christ, we almost always come for the worst possible reasons.

But notice what happens next—this is very important. *The father doesn't care!* He really doesn't care what brought the boy back home; he's just thrilled to see him. He doesn't walk to meet his son; he runs! Does he accept him back because the son has repented? No!

It's crystal clear. One day the father sees his son coming down the road toward home—and the son still hasn't changed. He's still a hobo, still a bum. Dad smells his ragamuffin son afar off, yet he still runs and embraces him and welcomes him before the boy can confess or make any kind of statement.

The son is accepted, you see. It's as simple as that. His father accepts him—period. He starts to blubber an excuse, but the father interrupts him. Verse 20:

> But while he was still a long way off, his father saw him and was filled with compassion for him; he ran to his son, threw his arms around him and kissed him. The son said to him, "Father, I have sinned against heaven and against you. I am no longer worthy to be called your son." But the father said to his servants, "Quick! Bring the best robe and put it on him. Put a ring on his finger and sandals on his feet. Bring the fattened calf and kill it. Let's have a feast and celebrate. For this son of mine was dead and is alive again; he was lost and is found."

## A modern prodigal

Philip Yancey tells the story of a young girl in Traverse City, Michigan, who decided her dad was stupid and her mom was stupid and home was stupid and church was stupid. She ran away to Detroit and ended up a druggie, earning a living by turning tricks like other homeless girls do. She was sleeping on metal grates outside department stores through the hard Detroit winter. Finally, she decided to call home. Three times in a row she got the answering machine. "Dad, Mom, it's me. I was wondering about maybe coming home. . . . I'm catching a bus up that way. It'll get there about midnight tomorrow. If you're not there . . . well, I guess I'll just stay on the bus until it gets to Canada."

She rode for seven hours on the bus. She worried and practiced her speech: "I've been so foolish. Can you ever forgive me?" The bus got closer to home. Her heart was pounding. *What if they never even got the message? What if they're not there?*

The bus rolled into Traverse City. "Fifteen minutes, folks!" the driver announced. Fifteen minutes to decide her life. Pure terror! She checked her hair and licked the lipstick off her teeth. According to the math of the world she ought to get nothing—zip—and she knew it. No forgiveness, no welcome back, no making up for how she had slapped everyone in the face.

She walked into the terminal, never in her wildest dream expecting to see what was there. There in the terminal stood forty people—brothers, sisters, great-aunts and uncles, cousins, a grandmother, and a great-grandmother! They were all wearing goofy party hats and blowing noisemakers. There was a huge banner taped across the entire terminal, "Welcome home!" *And there came her dad and mom!* Her eyes filled with tears, and she began the memorized speech, "Dad, I'm sorry."

"I know," he interrupted her. "Hush! We've got no time for that. You'll be late for the party! A banquet's waiting for you at home!"

You see, in Jesus' story, the father is more prodigal than the son. *Prodigal* means "overly lavish," "extravagant," "recklessly generous," "wasteful." And the real prodigal in Jesus' story is the father. He's outrageously generous. He gives away the family fortune, and then when the son comes home, he hands him the bank account again! The father has undiminished love for both his sons.

God's grace. We can never fully understand it—although it is a wonderful subject to examine and consider and explore. We can know more and more about it, but we will never fully understand it. In the following chapters of this book, we'll look at God's grace through the words of a beautiful hymn; we'll gain some insights that will be tremendously encouraging and helpful. But the best way to understand God's grace is to experience it. May this book help each of us to do just that—experience God's grace in our lives in a greater way than we have ever experienced it before.

\* \* \* \* \*

*Thank You, Lord, for being the Good Shepherd. When we stray, You search. When we hide, like the lost coin from the woman, You sweep away the concealing problems and celebrate our discovery. Like the loving father, when You see us making the slightest effort to return to You, You rush toward us and engulf us in Your grace. Thank You, Lord, for Your amazing grace to us! Amen.*

# CHAPTER TWO

# God's Greatest Gift

It's probably one of the most chilling sensations in the world. You're driving along in your car—an open freeway, clear nighttime driving conditions, cheerful, absorbing music blaring out through all four speakers, all eight cylinders zipping you along. You're having a great time.

All of a sudden you look in your mirror. And that red light is there!

That terrifying, imperious red light. You can't see the rest of the patrol car; you can't see the police officer—not yet. Just that glowing red light, all the power of that red light.

And you know you're had. Man, you were doing seventy-five, maybe even eighty. You just weren't thinking about it.

It hits you right in the stomach. It's actually a physical sensation, a sick feeling. This is going to cost you maybe two hundred bucks. Plus traffic school—at least here in California. Maybe even a little jump in your insurance rates. That red light in your rearview mirror means nothing but never-ending heartbreak.

17

The patrolman comes up; he's very courteous, very professional. He looks at your driver's license and your registration. There's a long moment while you just . . . *wait.*

And then, all of a sudden, he looks down at you and says, "Mr. Melashenko, I'm not going to give you a ticket this time. But please slow down, OK?"

You're off the hook! No ticket. No traffic school. No punishment. No insurance problems. You've been forgiven.

Friend, what you've experienced right there is *grace.* And that wonderful feeling of relief and freedom is just a tiny slice of the grace—God's grace—that we want to discuss in this book.

If you were to do a Top-Ten survey of favorite religious songs around the world, the song "Amazing Grace," I think, would show up on many, many lists. There is something about that quiet Christian gospel song that stirs a person's heart.

"Amazing Grace." Where does that song get its power? Why do so many people love it and point to it as a kind of life anchor, even a turning point for them?

Back in 1990, Bill Moyers produced a film for PBS with that very simple title: *Amazing Grace.* This beautiful documentary took cameras around North America and even overseas, looking for the song "Amazing Grace." From the country-twang back hills of Virginia to a boy's opera choir in the mean streets of New York City to ethnic singing groups in Asia, Moyers captured on film what that old song, "Amazing Grace," means to so many people.

The Moyers film made its public debut at RCC '90, a convention gathering of 2,000 religious communicators in Nashville. At a late-evening showing, hundreds of writers and PR practitioners for many faith groups sat and watched this film, *Amazing Grace.*

As you watched, you couldn't help but think of the rich meaning of the lines of that song: "Amazing grace, how sweet the sound, / that saved a wretch like me. / I once was lost, but now am found. / Was blind, but now I see."

You know, friend, there's a sermon hidden in every line of that song, "Amazing Grace." What's so amazing about it? What's the big deal about grace "that saved a wretch like me"? Are you and I really wretches? That's a harsh word; but does it apply? And then the line, "I once was lost." What about that?

I'll tell you something—grace becomes even more amazing when you simply stop and think about it. The song "Amazing Grace" and the concept of amazing grace both grow into something very precious in your heart.

There are actually at least six verses to this hymn, but just looking at the first stanza opens up rich meaning, such a precious picture of Jesus.

Let's take a brief moment together and think about the word *grace.* What really is grace? Why has this biblical concept become such an important pillar in the Christian faith?

Well, Webster's Dictionary lists eight definitions just of the *noun* part of grace. Of course, we think of "saying grace at meals," or maybe the title of a duke: "Your Grace."

But the definition that changes the world is this one: "Unmerited divine assistance given to humanity." Most Christian preachers, including yours truly, like to say simply: "Grace is unmerited favor." Getting something wonderful from God that we don't deserve. The New Testament Greek word *charis* carries the idea of "goodwill" or "favor."

*Salvation*—by which we mean having eternal life with Jesus and all God's people—is something we don't deserve. Not one citizen on this planet deserves to live. There is not one member of the human race who doesn't have a deserved death sentence hanging over his or her head.

A little girl was once asked what grace was. "Please, sir," she said, "it is getting everything for nothing." Not a bad definition, but a better one has been pointed out. If she'd said, "It is somebody who *deserves everything bad,* getting everything good for nothing," that would have been closer to the truth.

Romans, chapter three, contains the classic bad news/good news pronouncement of all time: "All have sinned and fall short of the glory of God" (verse 23).

There aren't any exceptions to that rule. Putting it bluntly, we're all in the driver's seat of that car on the freeway, and the red light is shining in through the back window. We're guilty. That's the bad news.

Friend, thank goodness there is a verse 24! Listen to the good news: "And are justified freely by his grace through the redemption that came by Christ Jesus."

And you really can't pen a book about grace without pointing out Ephesians 2:8, 9:

It is by grace you have been saved, through faith—and this not from yourselves, it is the gift of God—not by works, so that no one can boast.

Let's explore just two words in one phrase of the gospel song: *"That saved* a wretch like me." Paul tells us in Ephesians that it is grace that saves us. God's grace, God's undeserved favor, has the power to save. It's a gift from God. We can't earn it; we can't buy it; we can't qualify for it; we can't deserve it. And we certainly can't boast about the fact that we have it.

You know, when I've got that patrolman's flashlight in my eyes, and the red light strobing through my window, and the policeman says, "Lonnie, I'm going to let you off"—my best move at that moment is to just quietly say, "Thank you." That's not a very smart time to boast or honk my own horn. A quiet, "Thank you" is really the only appropriate response.

I think by the end of this book, you and I are going to find ourselves saying "Thank you" a lot. "Thank You, Lord, for the gift of amazing grace."

# CHAPTER THREE

# Grace That Saved

Here in Southern California, about fifty miles north of our *Voice of Prophecy* studio, are the Santa Barbara beaches. Now the surfing's not spectacular there, but just about 365 days a year you can see somebody in the water, waiting for a wave to come along. In the summer, a pair of cutoff jeans; in the winter, a wetsuit. Usually.

Jerome was your typical surfer—kind of a risk taker. He'd been catching waves for almost ten years, when one day the moment came that every surfer dreads. The wrong kind of a wipeout happened; his board flew up, hit him on the head, and dazed him.

He found himself underwater, sand and cold, greenish water swirling all around him. And he could feel the rip tide pulling at him—but he was paralyzed, helpless to do anything. He managed to struggle to the surface once, just as another vicious wave broke right over him and drove him down again. He simply couldn't move to save himself.

Even though he was physically dazed, his mind was still working. He could sense with awful terror that

22

death was upon him. He was going to drown. He'd always thought about death as an unreal thing, something *out there,* happening to others. Now it was about to happen to him. It was cold; it was horrible. He wanted to scream, but he was under the surface in this terrible green prison of Pacific Ocean water—about to die.

All at once he felt strong arms around him. Somehow a lifeguard had managed to come and rescue him.

Jerome was saved. Instead of dying, he lived. Instead of the blackness of drowning, he soon found himself on the beach with a blanket around him and a cup of hot chocolate in his hand. He felt a wonderfully safe feeling of having been rescued from the clutches of death itself.

Friend, that's a beautiful word, isn't it? *Saved.* To be saved. Or the word *safe.* It has a comforting feeling to it; it makes you think of blankets and hot chocolate and a mother's arms around you. A good solid lock on the door and a protector at your side.

You know, it's a funny thing. Christians talk about "being saved." And yet, we attach more meaning to the word when it describes being pulled out of the cold Pacific Ocean, or being rescued from a burning apartment building. To be physically saved from danger means more to us somehow than to be spiritually saved for eternity.

Let's look at just two words found in the second line of this old Christian gospel song "Amazing Grace"— "That saved a wretch like me." Let's think about those two words: *That saved.*

We talked in chapter two about grace itself: unmerited favor, God's gift to you and His gift to me that we don't deserve. God's willingness to simply hand us eternal life because of what Jesus did for us on the cross of Calvary.

You know, there are many things that grace does. In fact, the song "Amazing Grace" provides quite a theological education. Think about the informative list we find in its lyrics.

What does grace do? Let's run down the list. Number One: It teaches our heart to fear. Number Two: It relieves those fears. Three: It brings us through dangers, toils, and snares. Four: It's brought us safe thus far. Five: We're told that grace will lead us home. There's more. Number Six: Grace will give us something wonderful to sing about for a minimum of ten thousand years. In fact, by then we'll have just barely started.

But better than all six of those reasons put together is this little two-word announcement: It saves.

You know, friend, I'm so glad that grace saves. I'm thankful for all the rest of this song, but thank God for those two words: *"That saved* a wretch like me."

I want to confess to you: I know about the saving power of grace in my own life and in my experience as a Christian pastor.

So many times in my own experience—growing up as the oldest of five boys on a farm in Saskatchewan, in my high-school years, during college and seminary, and even as a pastor and speaker for *The Voice of Prophecy* radio broadcast, I've had to fall on my knees with tears streaming down my face. Friend, I needed grace. In fact, I was desperate for the saving, healing power of grace in my life. I was lost without it. I was like Jerome, pounded by the overwhelming power of the waves, drowning. I needed the strong arms of the greatest of all lifeguards, Jesus.

We read in Ephesians 2:8: "It is by grace you have been saved, through faith—and this not from yourselves, it is the gift of God." Paul adds this in talking about God:

> Who has *saved* us and called us to a holy life— not because of anything we have done but because of his own purpose and grace. This grace was *given* us in Christ Jesus before the beginning of time (2 Timothy 1:9, emphasis supplied).

Friend, I've needed that gift. I've needed to be pulled out of the ocean of spiritual failure in my own life.

We had a precious young lady—Lena, from the Ukraine—come into our *Voice of Prophecy* office a while back. Two years earlier, my wife, Jeannie, and I and my parents were in Borislav, Ukraine, holding some Christian meetings. Lena was in attendance. Somehow, this precious young Russian girl understood the gospel message of grace and the gift of Jesus Christ through our translated messages. She accepted Jesus as her Savior.

Now here she stood in front of our *Voice of Prophecy* worship group and shared, in remarkably good English, her story, her expression of gratitude that God had saved her. He'd rescued her from a communist, atheistic culture where it was almost impossible to learn about Him. She literally felt like she'd been pulled from a burning building.

And you know something: I couldn't help but think back to Jerome, the teenager who was pulled out of the ocean. He might live another fifty or sixty years. You rescue a person from the flames of an apartment fire, and they'll enjoy a few more years of life—thirty, forty, maybe even fifty years. But in the end, a death of some kind will swallow them up again. Any such rescue is in reality, temporary, a fleeting stay of execution.

But the miracle of amazing grace had rescued Lena to live forever! The message of Calvary had saved her from the tragic, empty numbness of secular communism and spiritual ignorance and given her the privilege of living for those ten thousand years and beyond in the kingdom of God! I had tears in my eyes sitting there and listening to her tell her story.

*Saved* can be an empty word, almost a tired word, for some of us. Christians ask one another, "Are you saved?" Almost like, "Have a nice day." Itinerant preachers on the beach or out at Dodger Stadium shout at people going by, "Hey, man, are you saved?"

But then you meet a Lena. Then that word means something. Or you sense for yourself the feeling of rescue, when God pulls you from your own whirlpool of sin and slavery to deadly habits. Then it happens; the phrase, "That saved a wretch like me" becomes real.

# CHAPTER FOUR

# A Wretch Like Me

Back in the 1970s and 1980s, there was a Hollywood actor who made his living in a very gripping way. Richard Kiel was a big man, almost seven feet tall. He landed a continuing role in a number of James Bond films as well as a villain named "Jaws."

In these pictures, Richard Kiel had a set of dentures that didn't require Polident; what they needed was steel wool and a soldering gun! With his row of stainless steel teeth and his towering seven-foot frame, he was a menacing but inept, tongue-in-cheek hit man for the despotic enemies of Secret Agent 007.

In real life, though, Richard Kiel was a born-again Christian, who sometimes would be in attendance at meetings such as the National Religious Broadcasters convention, held every year in Washington, D.C.

When you'd see him from a great distance, he really looked about like anyone else. But I'll tell you something: when he came walking up close to you, all of a sudden you saw how huge this guy was. A big, tall giant of a man with his regular human smile and his two massive hands. Still a little bit scary, even if he wasn't looking to bite your head off.

But next to him, anyone else felt absolutely tiny! Puny! Being around Richard Kiel would fix your puffed-up ego in a hurry.

As we continue through the lyrics of "Amazing Grace," let's look at four words that are most likely not our favorites. "Amazing grace, how sweet the sound, that saved *a wretch like me."*

When you look at those words, "a wretch like me," you begin to think to yourself, "Maybe it's just that haunting *tune* I've loved all this time. I never really thought about the song referring to 'a wretch like me.'"

Friend, are you a wretch? Is your life wretched and ruined in sin?

It bothers us to answer "yes" to that question. I look in the mirror, and it's contrary to my nature to say, "Lonnie, you're a wretch. Your spiritual condition is miserable!"

First of all, most people don't really feel that wretched in their day-to-day lives, and then especially not in their spiritual lives.

Our *Voice of Prophecy* offices and radio studio are located in Simi Valley, California. It's a nice town. Clean streets, usually an uncrowded freeway, well-stocked grocery stores, low crime rate, nice residential suburbs and tract developments, temperature in the mid-seventies. There's nothing here to make me feel wretched.

And then in my case, there's the fact of being in the Lord's work. Going to seminary for training in the ministry. Pastoring a church week after week, having parishioners come up and say, "Oh, pastor, that was a wonderful sermon. Thank you so much." Et cetera, et cetera. And then being invited to speak on the radio. You know, it becomes hard for a person to feel very wretched under those conditions.

But the Bible has something to say to Mr. Feeling-pretty-good-about-himself Lonnie Melashenko. It's found in Romans 3:10: "There is no one righteous, not even one." In the familiar King James Version, it reads like this: "There is none righteous, no not one." The much newer Living Bible paraphrase says it this way: "No one is good—no one in all the world is innocent." Well, that may be triple overkill, but you get the point.

It's easy, perhaps, for many of us—you and me both—to think to ourselves, *Yes, I've sinned. But compared to some of the killers I see on the news every night, I'm not wretched. I'm not a crack mother; I'm not a prostitute. I go to church, and I'm faithful to my spouse. I've raised three good kids. These Bible verses really aren't meant for me as much as they are for someone else.*

Tempting thoughts? Admit it! They are! For both of us.

Oh, but remember something. Remember how short you feel when you stand next to Richard Kiel—"Jaws"? Just think how spiritually short and sinful and wretched you and I ought to feel as we get close to Jesus! As we draw near to Him each day, as we sense His righteousness, we start to understand what kind of people we really are.

In the book of Isaiah, we find this startling announcement: "All our *righteous* acts are like filthy rags" (Isaiah 64:6, emphasis supplied).

It's amazing. Even the good things we do are so stained with twisted, devious little motives, so colored with selfishness and ulterior designs, that they're compared to filthy rags. In fact, the Old Testament vernacular here is actually referring to the kinds of cloths or rags a woman would use during what the Bible would delicately describe as her "time of being unclean."

Friend, we're all wretches. All of us. We're united in our state of undeservedness.

Maybe you don't feel it. Maybe those verses don't penetrate with conviction to your heart. Friend, ask God to show it to you—your wretchedness, that is. How many times have faithful Christians found themselves abruptly in the gutter either figuratively or literally? We're all capable of worse evil than perhaps you dream possible right now. As one writer put it: "We all have thoughts that would shame hell."

There's not a person alive who can rise above these Bible indictments. *No one righteous—no, not one? That's not me!* a Christian minister says to himself. And then scandal strikes. A televangelist points to others as sinners and fallen heroes—and soon the headlines and tabloids scream out his name. None of us is immune.

We all can look at the faces on death row and the drug lords who enslave fourth graders with their cocaine powder and the hookers in the police wagon and say to ourselves, "There but for the grace of God go I." In the eyes of God, we're in that same paddy wagon ourselves. Our own sins mean that we need grace just as much as the worst serial killer.

The Bible tells us that it's only when we realize our wretched condition that salvation can begin. It was the publican in the temple praying, "God, have mercy on me, a sinner" (Luke 18:13), who received forgiveness. He was the one who got back on the right road, while the Pharisee standing ten feet away, who didn't think Romans 3:10 applied to him, was left out.

Right now, we need to recognize our need. Do I need a Savior? Yes. Do you? Yes. Are we really and truly wretches capable of the very worst sins? Yes, we are. Many among us have already proved it; the rest of us are sin-filled time bombs just waiting to go off.

Facing this fact—that line two of the song "Amazing Grace" applies to *us*—is the key. "That saved a wretch like me." Friends, that's *our* line. They're playing *our* song, aren't they?

# CHAPTER FIVE

# I Once Was Lost

*Lost.* It's one of the scariest words in the English language. To be *lost* almost *sounds* cold, doesn't it? A chilly wind. And lonely. To be lost.

I suppose every single person on this planet has a memory of being lost. Most of us, in our childhood, have at least one painful story in our computer data bank that we've never quite been able to delete. One experience where we were lost.

I remember, as if it were yesterday, one experience that happened to me. Our family was moving to California in 1964, bringing two cars across the country on the southern route across the United States. No intercom, no maps, late at night, and we teenage boys were taking turns driving in the second car in a strange city. Unexpectedly and all of a sudden, we were separated from the other car—lost, no money, no maps, and no idea where the other car was. Of course, there finally did come that wonderful moment when we were safe together again, reunited with Mom and Dad. We'll look later at the joy that comes from being found. But for now, let's keep our focus on that word—*lost.*

I suppose part of the fright that goes with being lost is the inherent danger that comes with that condition. *Lost* certainly goes with *fear,* doesn't it? By nature, those two are linked together. To be lost may mean to be lonely and cold. You might be out all night by yourself. You might be left in the woods for weeks. Friend, you might even die. *Lost* and *death* do often go together.

It seems as if every other TV movie made these days deals with someone who is lost and has to tramp through four days of snow in order to find rescue. Lostness is a universal condition.

Of course, when we think about the song "Amazing Grace" and those words "I once was lost, but now am found," we're talking about spiritual lostness. Being in a lost condition as far as eternal life is concerned. That's the real "being lost" that ought to concern us most of all.

You know, it's a funny thing. We discussed earlier that being saved from drowning seems a lot more important to us than being saved for heaven. And here we find the same experience. Being lost in the woods is absolutely terrifying, but being spiritually lost raises hardly a flicker of concern for most people.

It's safe to say that a person can be lost and not realize it. Have you ever experienced that? Have you ever driven blithely fifty miles down the wrong road with no idea that you were totally lost?

The same thing is true in the spiritual realm, isn't it? A person can be lost and have no idea of that fact. Millions of people haven't been near a map for so long that they just don't know they are lost. So, of course, there's no fear. No sensation of danger.

If you have no destination, no place to go—if eternity with God isn't your goal—then *lost* becomes an empty word. Do you recall this meaningful bit of exchange from the book *Alice in Wonderland?*

> "Would you tell me, please, which way I ought to go from here."
> "That depends a good deal on where you want to get to," said the Cat.
> "I don't much care where," said Alice.
> "Then it doesn't much matter which way you go," said the Cat.

That's a chilling statement, isn't it? To experience the kind of lostness where you don't even care.

In the spiritual world, though, it's equally true that you can know exactly where you are right now—and still be lost. You might be reading this while sitting on the beach in Florida. You know exactly where you are, and still you're a lost person.

You might be a housewife or a construction worker having lunch in Dallas reading these words during your break. You know where you are. You know your location. And you're lost.

But you know something? There's good news. The Bible is full of good news for those who are lost.

First of all, the lost can be found! The song "Amazing Grace" tells us that. The gift of grace was created specifically for those who are lost.

Friend, when they play "Amazing Grace," they're playing our song. Because God loves those who are lost; He gave His Son to die for those who are lost.

So many of Christ's stories have to do with something that was lost. The Shepherd who goes to look for His lost sheep. The woman who looks for the lost coin. The loving Father who goes out each day to look for the lost son—and rejoices when he is found.

Do you remember the childhood Bible story of Zacchaeus? He was a lost little man up there in that sycamore tree. And Jesus came looking for him. Jesus came to save him.

After Zacchaeus was found, Jesus made this wonderful pronouncement, this unforgettable mission statement: "The Son of Man came to seek and to save what was lost" (Luke 19:10).

Those who are lost are Jesus' target audience. They're the focus of His efforts, the prize He seeks to reclaim. If you're lost right now, He's looking for you.

And there's more good news. You may be lost right now, but it's possible to be found. You might be on the wrong road at this very moment, but there *is* a right road. And you can quickly get to there from where you are *right now*. There's an off-ramp coming up just ahead!

The great Christian writer, C. S. Lewis, wrote in his classic book *Mere Christianity:*

> We all want progress. But progress means getting nearer to the place where you want to be. And if you have taken a wrong turning, then to go forward does not get you any nearer. If you are on the wrong road, progress means doing an about-turn and walking back to the right road; and in that case the man who turns back soonest is the most progressive man.

And then he adds this: "We are on the wrong road. And if that is so, we must go back. Going back is the quickest way on."

"Amazing Grace" tells us that being lost is a temporary condition for those who ask for help. Someone very loving is looking for you right now.

# CHAPTER SIX

# But Now Am Found

The whole world watched in fingernail-biting anxiety as construction crews tried to rescue little Jessica McClure. Do you remember? Back in cold October of 1987, the story of the little eighteen-month-old girl trapped in a well in Midland, Texas, made headlines around the globe.

Little Jessica was lost in a certain kind of way—everybody knew where she was, but for fifty-eight agonizing hours her parents just couldn't get to her. Sometimes that's the hardest kind of being lost for a parent to take.

Throughout this book we've been letting the words to "Amazing Grace" give us new insights into God's dealings with you and me. We've taken a hard look at a hard topic—these four words: "I once was lost." And I know I took some comfort from realizing that later in the song we would have four much greater words to give us hope. "I once was lost . . . *but now am found.*"

As gut-wrenching as the word *lost* is, the word *found* is one of the most beautiful in the English language.

I'm sure in every language around the world, the word for *found* is one of the sweetest.

What a moment it is when the shouts go up from the rescue team, "We found her!" When the ski patrol finally comes across the lost victim up in the snow. When the helicopter finally plucks the last victim out of the freezing river. "We found him! The lost is found!"

It feels so good to *be* found, doesn't it? To be safe in Mom's arms again. To sit in the back seat of the car wrapped in a blanket and know that Dad is up front driving you to the safety of home, the warmth of your own bed. And especially when just an hour ago, you were lost. You were far away from home and from loved ones, facing loneliness and maybe even death. You were in the bottom of that well like little Jessica McClure. But now you're in your mother's arms again.

Friend, the Bible speaks with unabashed enthusiasm about the joy of finding that which was lost. Do you remember how the Good Shepherd leaves the ninety-nine sheep and goes to find the one that's lost? And when He does, what happens? He calls His friends and neighbors over and passes out refreshments and says to them, "Rejoice with me; I have found my lost sheep" (Luke 15:6).

We find the same thing in the parable of the lost coin. "Rejoice with me" (verse 9). And that's especially true in the precious parable of the prodigal son. Day after day the father is looking for him. While the bedraggled son is still "a long way off" (verse 20), the Bible says, "the father sees him and goes running to greet him." And then the celebration begins. Remember? "Bring the best robe! Kill the fatted calf! Pull out all the stops, you servants! My son was dead and now is alive! Lost . . . but now he's found!" (see verses 22-24).

The bottom line of this little trio of stories comes in verse seven: "I tell you," Jesus said to His disciples, ". . . there will be more rejoicing in heaven over one sinner who repents than over ninety-nine righteous persons who do not need to repent."

You may want to say, "Pastor Melashenko, that's parable talk. That's a lovely metaphor—'rejoicing in heaven'—but it's not real. There's not really a party in heaven over one person. Especially over me."

Friend, I beg to differ with you. This isn't simply sugar-coated poetic license or colorful metaphor-flavored literature; this is the truth! Friend, God knows you! He knows where you are right now. And His rejoicing is real at the very moment when you choose to be found.

Right here is the crucial point, the beautiful nuance of "Amazing Grace" that maybe you have missed up until now. The third line reads this way: "I once was lost, *but now am found.*"

Did you notice that? You didn't stumble back to civilization yourself; *Someone found you.* Someone came looking.

Many of the lost-and-found stories we see on network television happened when the lost party, by his or her own heroic measures, made it back to camp. And sometimes people talk about a kind of spiritual journey where they try to "find themselves."

Oh, but not here, friend! Here in "Amazing Grace," we find a loving God who does the finding. You don't get yourself un-lost; He comes and personally finds you!

You know, part of this process of salvation—in addition to discovering that we really are wretches and that we really are lost—is coming to the realization that we can't rescue ourselves. We're lost, and we can't get home by ourselves. The road is blocked; the telephone lines are down; we can't get across the swollen river. By our own efforts, we're not just lost, we're hopelessly lost. We're doomed in our lost condition.

But God comes looking! "I once was lost, but now am found." Just as in the story of the prodigal son, the Father is out looking for you. And while you're still a long way off, He sees you and comes running to the rescue. Here is what God says in Ezekiel 34:15, 16:

> "I myself will tend my sheep and have them lie down," declares the Sovereign Lord. "I will search for the lost and bring back the strays. I will bind up the injured and strengthen the weak."

The much-loved nineteenth-century Christian writer, E. G. White, penned these words in her classic book, *The Desire of Ages*: "Every soul is as fully known to Jesus as if he were the only one for whom the Saviour died."

He knows you! Just as the shepherd knows his sheep, He knows you. He knows who you are and where you are. If you're lost, He knows it. And He's on His way to rescue you right now. You may have been lost, but you can be found. Right now.

My good pastor friend Morris Venden has written a book entitled *Hard to Be Lost*. It's hard to be lost, he suggests, when God is looking so hard for you. It's hard to be lost when so many people are praying for you. It's hard to be lost when all the armies of heaven have devoted themselves to this one rescue—yours!

Have you ever played the board game "Sorry"? Your four little green men or blue men are out there on the board, vulnerable and lost. Even when you get them into your own row marked *Safety,* sometimes you still lose them. You get a "Backward 4" card and have to back out into the alleyway of danger.

But finally comes that sweet moment when you take them all the way into *Home.* Safely home! Now no one can take them out of that haven; no one can take them and say, "Sorry." When you're home, everything is safe and secure.

Right now, you can go home. Not alone; no one can make it home alone. But because of the amazing grace displayed at Calvary, and because we have a good Shepherd and a loving Father who have formed a rescue party, home is very near. In fact, it's just around the corner; it's right up ahead. And the rescue team is running toward you!

# CHAPTER SEVEN

# I Was Blind

It's one of the horrible words in the English language—*blind*. To be *blind*.

British author C. S. Lewis once remarked how certain words take on a painful power of their own—the word *haunted,* for instance. And how even a child who doesn't know the meaning of the word *haunted* will shudder if he hears an adult say, "That house is haunted."

*Blind* seems to carry that same kind of jolt. Try to imagine being blind.

"Amazing grace, how sweet the sound, / that saved a wretch like me. / I once was lost, but now am found." And then we come to six very memorable words: "Was blind, but now I see."

First, let's look at just two of those six words: *was blind.* You and I, as subjects of this song, "Amazing Grace," have experienced blindness. A certain kind of blindness, more deadly and dark than even the loss of physical sight. Spiritual blindness. A moral blackness where we can't see our way out.

You know, the book of Revelation has a message for

the church of Laodicea, the church of the last days—
in other words, you and me. And you remember what
it says:

> You say, "I am rich; I have acquired wealth
> and do not need a thing." But you do not realize
> that you are wretched, pitiful, poor, *blind,* and
> naked (Revelation 3:17, emphasis supplied).

Notice what it says. Blind, but not realizing it. We're
not seeing, and we don't know that we're not seeing!
We think we *are* seeing! We think we've got 20/20 vision. We haven't even made an appointment with the
optometrist because we don't think we need to. "I can
see just fine, thank you anyway."

Friend, what is it that we're not seeing? What is it
that our blindness is causing us to miss?

Well, the fact that we find this line—"Was blind,
but now I see"—in the song "Amazing Grace," should
be our biggest clue. It's grace itself that we're not
seeing. For thousands and maybe millions of church-
going, Bible-believing, tithe-paying, professing be-
lievers—we're blind to the idea that we really do
need Jesus. We can't see that all our goodness doesn't
count for anything and that we need the gift of amazing grace.

Let me confess again as I did earlier: I've fallen often into the trap of not realizing that I'm wretched,
pitiful, poor, naked, and blind. I've been tempted to
look at my résumé and my theological degrees and for-
get about my need of grace. I've awakened in the morning and found myself in spiritual blindness, not seeing my desperate need of Jesus and Calvary.

Working at *The Voice of Prophecy,* I travel to a lot of religious meetings where Christians from a whole region will gather for several days or a weekend. And I've encountered folks who have gone to these meetings for fifty years; they've sat in the pews of their church back home every weekend for fifty years—and they haven't accepted the Bible truth of grace. In their own blinded vision, they believed they had demonstrated a kind of faithfulness and obedience on their own that qualified them for eternal life. I know because they told me so.

Friend, there's an enemy out there who is trying to blind us. To keep us from catching even a glimpse of grace. To keep us from seeing God and to cause us to see instead a distorted, unfocused, fuzzy picture of Him. Because even worse than blindness is to see falsehood.

How many people have believed lies about God and ended up in spiritual blindness? Friend, maybe your blindness has come upon you because somebody out there lied to you about God. Perhaps God was portrayed as your enemy, your everlasting tormentor, your executioner. Maybe grace was buried beneath a blanket of rules and human obedience. And you believed the "lies"—the misrepresentations—they told you. What they told you wasn't true, but you thought it was, and that blindness kept you paralyzed. You were a slave, blind and imprisoned because of believing a lie.

I'm glad that God doesn't hold us accountable for our blindness and the blankets that have blocked out the sunlight. He doesn't hold us accountable—unless we refuse to accept the eye salve He provides.

"Was blind, but now I see." You see, God promises us that there is a cure for blindness. All through the New Testament, Jesus healed blindness. In the Revelation verses we just mentioned, Jesus promises eye salve, healing ointment, to those who will accept it. Your blindness can be healed; you can see His grace again. In fact, He Himself is the eye salve you need. He says, "For judgment I have come into this world, so that the blind will see" (John 9:39).

Yes, Jesus Himself is the self-described Light of the world, the Light that penetrates and conquers our darkened vision.

We've been looking at the biblical topic of grace—at the fact that Jesus came down from a throne in heaven to this dirty little planet. He came down here to live among people like you and me. He came down here knowing He was going to die. He came down here knowing He was going to be rejected and persecuted and ridiculed and killed. But He did it anyway so that something called grace could be our rescue. Grace. Amazing grace.

Actually, grace is not just amazing; it's more than amazing. We read about some tremendous scientific discovery. Astronauts have just tried some feat that hasn't been accomplished before, or researchers may have a breakthrough against a certain disease. And all the TV commentators say the same thing—"Amazing!"

Friend, if those things are amazing, then Calvary is more than amazing. If the headlines on TV are amazing, then we really need a new song to sing, entitled, "More-Than-Amazing Grace."

*Amazing* is a good word. Grace *is* amazing, and we need to daily be amazed by grace. But if grace and

Calvary and Jesus' sacrifice for us are on the same emotional level as many of the "amazing" things that happen in our world day by day, then we need to think again and either find some deeper word or a deeper love for the gift of grace.

I love how the apostle Paul describes the package plan that is grace:

> Being in very nature God, [Jesus Christ] did not consider equality with God something to be grasped, but made himself nothing, taking the very nature of a servant, being made in human likeness. And being found in appearance as a man, he humbled himself and became obedient to death—even death on a cross! Therefore God exalted him to the highest place and gave him the name that is above every name, that at the name of Jesus every knee should bow, in heaven and on earth and under the earth, and every tongue confess that Jesus Christ is Lord, to the glory of God the Father (Philippians 2:6-11).

There it is. Jesus came from the very highest point the universe could know, down here to the very lowest point a person could conceive. And now He occupies the highest point again, where He offers His own blood, His own creation of grace, for you and for me. That's how Paul saw it; that's how more than amazing he thought God's grace was.

In fact, in his letter to the Christians at Galatia, Paul wrote this: "May I never boast except in the cross of our Lord Jesus Christ" (Galatians 6:14).

Actually, he goes even further. When he wrote his first letter to the Corinthians, Paul essentially said, "I don't even want to know about anything except the cross" (see 1 Corinthians 2:2). For Paul, it was Calvary that was amazing. Human achievements weren't amazing; military victories weren't amazing. The accomplishment of people—even his own little list of successes—weren't amazing. Paul thought that what Jesus had done in dying for him—that was amazing.

Are we all that excited about what Jesus has done for us? Are we that excited about amazing grace?

So much of what we call "amazing" is incredibly temporary. Today's headlines are gone tomorrow. Today's little accomplishment is forgotten by next weekend. But the gift of grace is forever! It lasts beyond the weekend, beyond next year, beyond the centuries, beyond time itself on this planet. God's grace survives for eternity.

It really is amazing—this more-than-amazing grace. So why do we find it so difficult at times to see it clearly and recognize just how amazing God's grace really is? Perhaps your blindness has been that of limited vision. You can see—but not very far. You've glimpsed grace—but not very much of it. You know God has power—but somehow you've not seen it being very active in your life. You've read and heard all your life that Jesus is coming soon—but you've stopped seeing that promised event as being very real.

Even at this very moment, you may feel surrounded by enemy forces. The devil's been after you with temptation and discouragement. Your little battle station is surrounded by hostile forces; you feel like General

Custer or like the servant of the Bible prophet Elisha who cried out to his boss: "Alas, master, what shall we do? The Arameans are all around us!" (see 2 Kings 6:8-16).

And, you know, Elisha prayed: "Lord, open his eyes" (verse 17). That servant looked up, and his blindness was removed. Instantly, he saw the hosts of heaven's armies and the chariots of fire all around them, ready to do battle on their behalf.

Friend, those very same armies are still there! They haven't gone into military retirement. The same angels and the same God are present in your life today. Calvary and grace are still here with you, surrounding you. It's time to open your eyes and see them—really see them.

"Was blind but now I see."

# CHAPTER EIGHT

# Now I See

Thomas had been blind all his life. For more than fifty years—half a century—he'd known nothing but the intense blackness of his handicap. He'd never known anything but that darkness.

And then came the day when a world-renowned surgeon, following hours of delicate ophthalmic surgery, gently removed the bandages covering Thomas's eyes. There was one agonizing moment of tension and suspense. Would the patient, after all these years, be able to see again?

Thomas, his heart pounding in his chest, blinked twice, then opened his eyes. And there it all was—the blue sky outside, the curtains on the windows, the faces of his parents and friends, all the colors on the wallpaper, and the trees outside. And, of course, the smile of the surgeon as he viewed the incredible results of his successful labor.

"Was blind, but now I see." Certainly, as we consider all the lyrics of the gospel song "Amazing Grace," these four words—"but now I see"—have to be among the most poignant. What a miracle to see again after being blind!

49

Most of us don't think a whole lot about walking, but have you ever walked after being lame? Have you listened to a symphony or the roar of a waterfall after being deaf for thirty or forty years?

The closest you and I will probably come to this experience is when we're sick and in bed and then finally are well again and get up to enjoy life once more. What a marvelous sensation—to feel good! To be well after such a long time of feeling miserable!

But nothing can beat the miracle of seeing again when you were blind before. Seeing is such an all-powerful, all-encompassing, life-altering sense. And to have it when you didn't have it before—so few people have ever had that experience.

You know, to be blind and to be lost kind of go together, don't they. They go together in daily life and in our spiritual lives as well. A blind person is going to lose his or her way.

But, friend, it's equally true, and wonderfully true, that to see again is to also be found again. What wonderful news in heaven when a lost person is found! And that rescue mission reaches fulfillment when a blind person is brought at last to the point of sight. When the darkness of not seeing amazing grace is shattered by the searchlight shining down from Calvary. What a great moment that is!

My friend, pastor Mark Finley, who serves as the speaker of our sister broadcast, the *It Is Written* TV program, tells how he once met a young woman named Marcia during a series of meetings. At these meetings she found Jesus and started living life all over again with Him.

She wrote a note to Pastor Finley later, and it went like this:

> Dear Pastor Finley: How could I have been so blind? How could I have been so stupid? I spent thirty-one years just running. Looking for something. I didn't know what. My philosophy was go, go, go. I've never been able to sit down and relax; I've just been running from place to place, taking pills to calm me down, more pills to get to sleep, drinking a glass of wine, trying to relax.
>
> Feeling so alone. I never understood what inner peace was! For the first time in my life, Jesus has captured my heart. I'm not alone anymore. He loves me! He died so I could be forgiven. What a shame I never loved Him before! Thank You, Jesus, for loving me. I'm so glad I'm not alone anymore.

How can you top that? One letter like that keeps you going for a long time. It really does. And we get mail like that at *The Voice of Prophecy* every single day. People who pour out their hearts on beautiful perfumed stationery or on the back of a cocktail napkin: "Now I get it! All my life I couldn't see it; people tried to tell me, and I just didn't get it. I was blind, but now I see." Somehow, some way, the Holy Spirit finds His way through to the heart and the eyes—the spiritual eyes.

Friend, right now I'd like to share two important points with you.

We've explored the beautiful truth that when we're lost, we don't find our own way home. The Father comes looking for us.

And we've seen that when we're blind, we can't make ourselves see again. We need healing from an outside source! We need the eye salve that Jesus provides.

And yet, God so often provides the miracle of restored sight through others.

Do you remember the Bible story found in John's Gospel, in which Jesus healed a man who was blind from birth? Jesus took a dab of dirt, a bit of saliva, and some of the water from the Pool of Siloam to aid in the healing process.

Today, just as God may work through the talented, loving hands of an eye surgeon to bring you physical sight, He uses His servants, His people, even His church, to restore spiritual sight to those who are blind.

Think back through your own life, and right now I'll do the same thing. Think of people who have prayed for you: parents, school teachers, maybe a godly church member or teacher. Think of people who have opened up the Bible for you and showed you the truth. God used them as His appointed eye surgeons, didn't He?

I can remember good books that my mom and dad gave me for Christmas and for my birthday. I can think of nine million times that my wife, Jeannie, has been used by God to show me the gift of grace. Her prayers for me, her loving words of encouragement—God's used her to point me over and over toward Calvary. Praise God for a good Christian spouse.

Maybe somebody sent you a letter when you were discouraged. Or, friend, maybe during a moment of darkness, a time of near blindness for you, you turned on your radio or television and you heard someone speaking for God—a sermon or a Bible message—and God used them to bring you out of darkness and into

the light. Isn't it marvelous how God works through
His servants?

Right now, maybe He'd like to use you. Maybe you're
walking in the light, and your son or daughter or your
neighbor is blind. How about it? Is there a letter you
could write or a phone call you could make right now?
A prayer you could whisper?

That's my challenge for you, and I'm writing a note
to myself as well. "Lonnie, this is for you too." I'm not
just a radio program host. I've got neighbors and rela-
tives and lonely, blind people who come into my life as
well. I want God to use me to turn on the spotlight
and let them see the grace that flows from Calvary.

One more brief point. The blind man Jesus healed
caused quite a stir among the Pharisees and priests.
And they asked him: "Who did this?"

"Jesus," the man answered enthusiastically.

That didn't make them very happy. "This Jesus is a
sinner. He's not from God," they insisted.

Listen to this marvelous reply from the man who
was seeing the light of day for the very first time.
"Whether he is a sinner or not, I don't know. One thing
I do know. I was blind but now I see!" (John 9:25).

The healing, the return of that man's sight, was proof
to him that Jesus was real! That Jesus was the Messiah, the giver of grace. Because he saw again, he believed.

You know something? Two thousand years later, the
same logic works again. When you finally see grace,
you believe in the Provider of that grace. Our restored
vision is the proof we need, the answer to all our ques-
tions. So many Christians are walking around praising God because they can see again. That miracle gives

validation to the claims of Jesus Christ to be your Savior right now.

A little boy went to summer camp and was having a bad time. The other kids picked on him because he was small and clumsy and because he talked funny, with a kind of thick slowness. The boys in his cabin called him "Retard" until he was almost in tears.

Then a Christian counselor took that little boy and told him a story. It was a story about a cross and a Man named Jesus. This kid had never heard that story before.

Well, the next day the teasing and the meanness started up again. But this time the boy just stood there and looked at his attackers. There were no tears this time. Then everybody heard it. Just two words that echoed through the hills of that campsite and down to the lake. Two words came from that boy with his slow, clumsy speech.

"Good news!"

Nobody knew what to say to that. "Good news!" It was a cry of triumph. A shout of in-your-face victory. Somebody had told that persecuted little guy some good news. Somebody had told him how much he was worth to Heaven.

"Good news! I once was blind, but now I see."

# CHAPTER NINE

# More Than Amazing Grace

In most hymnals, it's just thirty-five notes long. You can play it or sing it in fewer than thirty seconds. There's nothing complicated or musically challenging about this very straightforward song written in three-quarter time.

What *is* it, then, about this song, "Amazing Grace"? Why does the tune have such power to bring tears to a strong man's eyes?

A few years ago, thousands of young people were at a rock concert. Huge banks of amplifiers and speakers lined the stage; it was a zillion-decibel-powerhouse evening featuring a number of popular bands.

Out in the audience, the kids were swaying to the music, feeling the hard-driving rhythm. And, of course, just like at most rock performances, there was marijuana smoke in the air. The tequila and beer were flowing freely. Promiscuity and sexual liberty were part of the hazy atmosphere.

Then suddenly things grew quiet. Opera star Leontyne Price walked to center stage and stood there alone. No guitar. No backup band. No laser lights or special effects.

And she began to sing. "Amazing grace, how sweet the sound, / that saved a wretch like me . . . "

And all through that huge cavernous hall, it got quiet. All those kids suddenly stood in their tracks and listened. "I once was lost, but now am found. Was blind, but now I see." It was a transforming moment.

Why? What is it about this song?

Earlier in this book, I told you about the film by Bill Moyers—*Amazing Grace,* the PBS documentary. Moyers and a camera crew traveled around the world looking at beautiful vignettes describing how this song means more than life itself to those who sing it. Country people living out in the hills, gathering together at a little white church every Sunday morning. An urban choir of black elementary schoolboys from New York City who circle the globe singing "Amazing Grace" with Broadway precision.

Everyone involved in the documentary film testified that there was power in the song "Amazing Grace." Something indefinable, something mysterious and wonderful about the notes, the tune, and especially the message. Grace—unmerited favor. God's gift of grace to this weary, sin-sick planet.

I want to confess to you: I love that song. Ever since I was a boy growing up in Canada, I've loved "Amazing Grace." My four brothers and I have sung it together many times. It does have a sweetness and a power that move me.

But I want to say this—as sweet as the tune for "Amazing Grace" is, grace itself is even sweeter. And I want to challenge you right now: Don't let the beauty of the music overshadow the saving message of "Amazing Grace."

I think back to those kids at that rock concert. They stood there in sober silence, listening to the quiet melody of "Amazing Grace." And I'm sure many of them had their hearts touched by the haunting beauty of those thirty-five notes. They probably turned to their girlfriends and said, "Wow, that's something. That really got to me."

But then a moment later the rock and roll started up again, and the sweetness of that one tune was lost. The song was sweet, but they missed the greater sweetness, the lasting power of *grace* itself.

I don't want that to happen to me. It's possible to sing "Amazing Grace" in church. It's so beautiful; you feel so close to Jesus at that moment. You want to love Him and serve Him and have a relationship with Him.

And then you go out to the parking lot and see that someone has scratched your car. Or somebody cuts you off as you pull out onto the freeway. And all your sweet feelings from that beautiful tune are gone. You allowed the music to be sweeter than the grace.

Friend, it's the grace itself that has the power to change your life forever. A haunting melody lasts only as long as the notes linger in the air and in your memory. But a knowledge of grace itself—Calvary and of a Savior named Jesus Christ—that can last for always. *It's grace that saves your life, not the tune "Amazing Grace."*

There's no person beyond the reach of the power of grace. Maybe you've heard the story of John Newton, who made his living in probably the lowest way imaginable. He was the captain of a slave ship.

I want you to think about that for a minute—captain of a slave ship. Transporting human beings, men and women and boys and girls, in the hold of your ship. Kidnapping people and dragging them away, screaming, from their families. Packing them like cramped sardines in the damp bowels of your ship, alternating them head to toe in the oxygen-starved darkness, knowing full well that half of them will die before reaching the shores of North America. And then sitting in your comfortable captain's quarters with paper and a quill pen, callously calculating to yourself that even with that 50 percent morality rate, even with half of your cargo being thrown overboard before you reach your destination, you can still turn a profit.

It was an evil and depraved way to make a living. But that was the world of John Newton. He made his money, his livelihood, bartering in human cargo. John Newton had sold his very soul, sinking as low as a man could go; he had chosen as despicable and cruel a path as a man can walk.

And somehow the miracle of grace reached down to John Newton. If ever a man were lost, it was he. If ever a man were blind to the anguish and misery around him, it was John Newton. Blind to the saving power of Jesus Christ.

Somehow grace got through to John Newton. He encountered Jesus Christ. He came face-to-face with Calvary and with his own opportunity for salvation.

It wasn't the tune of "Amazing Grace" that saved John Newton. It was amazing grace itself.

You see, and perhaps you already knew, it was John Newton who picked up that same quill pen with which he figured his profits in human lives and wrote the gospel song we all know and love—"Amazing Grace!" John Newton, repentant slave-ship captain, looked back at where he'd been and wrote, "I once was lost, but now am found. Was blind, but now I see." And it was John who wrote the lines of another verse we haven't even mentioned: "How precious did that grace appear, the hour I first believed."

Maybe it's hard to believe that something as sweet sounding as grace would have the power to reach a John Newton. Listen, friend, for all its sweet tenderness, grace has an amazing raw power. Listen to how Paul describes it:

> For I am convinced that neither death nor life, neither angels nor demons, neither the present nor the future, nor any powers, neither height nor depth, nor anything else in all creation, will be able to separate us from the love of God that is in Christ Jesus our Lord (Romans 8:38, 39).

That's the gutsy power of God's amazing grace. Nothing can stop it or even slow it down. It reached clear down to where John Newton was. It reached down to where I was. Right now, it's reaching out to you—right where you are, right now.

# CHAPTER TEN

# It's Your Choice

In this little book, we've been looking at God's amazing grace—what it means and how it can affect our lives. But now we've come to the final chapter. Now we've come to the place where we need to do more than just talk about God's amazing grace. We've come to the place where we need to *do* something about it.

You see, God's grace truly is amazing. But it can't accomplish anything amazing for you unless you accept that grace of God into your own life. The Bible says, "As many as received Him [Jesus], to them He gave the right to become children of God" (John 1:12, NKJ). We've got to receive that grace into our lives to receive God's power and salvation.

It's like the electricity coming into your home. There is an electrical generating station somewhere in your city or area, and that station is filled with thousands and thousands of watts of electrical power. That power is delivered along the power grid and through smaller and smaller lines until at last there is a line that reaches your house. All that power is waiting outside.

It's there just waiting to go to work for you and make all kinds of good things happen in your house. But unless you actually turn on the switch—unless you actually invite the power into your home—nothing is going to happen.

That's the way it is with God's grace—His saving power. Heaven is filled with God's power to save and change your life. But until you invite Him in, until you actually reach out and accept the power of His grace, your life is going to remain the same. But, friend, when you accept God's grace, amazing things happen! You are changed from death to life!

One of the most well-known and well-loved verses in the Bible says, "For God so loved the world that He gave His only begotten Son, that whoever believes in Him should not perish but have everlasting life" (John 3:16, NKJ). That's a wonderful declaration of God's love; a wonderful promise of salvation to all who believe. That's why it is probably the most-loved verse of Scripture. But have you ever thought of what it is saying between the lines?

It is saying that if we do *not* believe, if we do *not* accept Jesus as our Savior, we will perish instead of living forever. Does that sound like the God of love we have been talking about in this book?

Yes. You see, God is love. Nothing in the Bible is clearer than that. But He is also fair and just. He tells it like it is, and the truth is that sin cannot exist in His presence. A time is coming when sin will be destroyed, and if we insist on remaining attached to it, we will be destroyed along with it.

If God had His way, if the decision were entirely up to Him, no one would be lost. But the decision is ultimately yours and mine. God has done everything possible to ensure our salvation. He invites us to accept His amazing grace. But if we refuse, He can do nothing more. His Word clearly lays out the choice we each have to make: life or death. Mercy or judgment. Vindication or condemnation. The choice is ours, and God is too honest and too loving to tell us otherwise.

Let's review briefly what God says about your need for His amazing grace and what it can mean for your life.

- The Bible says that God is love. It is this love—and nothing we have done—that caused Him to redeem us. *"God is love. In this the love of God was manifested toward us, that God has sent His only begotten Son into the world, that we might live through Him"* (1 John 4:8, 9, NKJ).

- We are all sinners—every human being who has ever lived upon the earth. *"All have sinned and fall short of the glory of God"* (Romans 3:23).

- Because of our sins we deserve to die—eternally. But God offers to give us the gift of eternal life through His amazing grace. *"The wages of sin is death, but the gift of God is eternal life in Christ Jesus our Lord"* (Romans 6:23).

- We receive His gift of eternal life by believing on Jesus and accepting Him as our Savior. *"For God so loved the world that He gave His only begotten Son, that whoever believes in Him should not perish but have everlasting life"* (John 3:16, NKJ).

- Jesus took our sins and died for them on the cross so that we could have His righteousness. *"He was wounded for our transgressions, He was bruised for our iniquities; the chastisement for our peace was upon Him, and by His stripes we are healed. . . . The Lord has laid on Him the iniquity of us all"* (Isaiah 53:5, 6, NKJ).

- If we ask Jesus to forgive us, he will. *"If we confess our sins, He is faithful and just to forgive us our sins and to cleanse us from all unrighteousness"* (1 John 1:9, NKJ).

- When we repent of our sins and, in faith, accept Jesus as our Savior, God gives us salvation as a free gift of His grace. *"By grace you have been saved through faith, and that not of yourselves; it is the gift of God, not of works, lest anyone should boast"* (Ephesians 2:8, 9, NKJ).

- In Jesus, we have salvation and eternal life now. *"God has given us eternal life, and this life is in His Son. He who has the Son has life; he who does not have the Son of God does not have life"* (1 John 5:11, 12).

If you have never accepted Jesus' offer of forgiveness and eternal life, perhaps He is asking you to make that decision right now. There will never be a better time. Just tell Him that you know you are a sinner. Tell Him that you believe He came to earth to be your Savior and that He died for your sins on the cross. Then tell Him that you accept the forgiveness He has promised.

Or you may have accepted Jesus at some time in your life, but you have since turned from Him to follow your own way. If so, He wants you to know that He will always take you back—no matter how long it's been or how far you have gone. Won't you ask Him to do just that, right now?

You may be a Christian, secure in God's amazing grace. If so, you know that living with Him is a matter of inviting Him into your life *daily*. Why not pause and thank Him right now for the salvation He has given you?

Friend, I hope that you have found Jesus in this little book. I hope you have come to see God's amazing grace in a new way. Remember, God loves you. His amazing grace is reaching out to you just now, offering you abundant life for today—a life that will last throughout eternity.

Won't you say "Yes"? The choice is yours.